# of CATS and Men

# of CATS and Men

PROFILES of HISTORY'S GREAT CAT-LOVING ARTISTS, WRITERS THINKERS and STATESMEN

SAM KALDA

TEN SPEED PRESS
California | New York

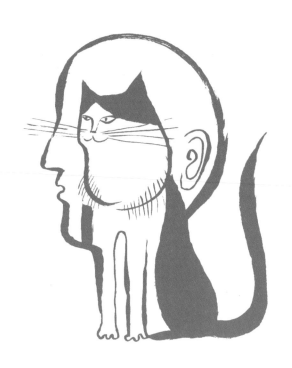

To my parents.

CONTENTS

WHEN A MAN I AM HIS FRIEND *without* INTROD

LOVES CATS, AND COMRADE, *further* UCTION.

Mark Twain

WHAT IS A CAT MAN?

Men are often portrayed in the company of dogs. They hunt together, run happily side by side, and ride shoulder to shoulder in mud-splattered pickups—the perfect image of masculine bliss. The dog is, after all, man's best friend. *Some* men, that is.

For centuries, legions of forward-thinking men—artists, writers, scientists, and philosophers—have shared their libraries and studios with a purring feline or two. In recent years, a new population of proud, cat-loving men has come out of the proverbial "cat closet," embracing the purr, mew, and squint of feline companionship.

Women have, for centuries, been chided and maligned for having *a* cat, let alone several. This "crazy cat lady" stereotype is deeply unfair. Like Prometheus to fire, generations of enlightened fellows have gravitated to the feline species. We stand with our cat-loving sisters as crazy cat men, proudly wearing our scarlet letters in solidarity.

Since man first discovered a fallen whisker in the forests of Eden, he has had a twilight bond with cats. We need only imagine the temples of ancient Egypt, where the priests prayed to statues of Bastet, cat goddess of the Egyptian people and protectress against disease and evil spirits. When a cat died, the Egyptians would shave their eyebrows in mourning—theirs was a truly cat-crazy culture. In fact, when a temple of Bastet was excavated in the late nineteenth century, archaeologists uncovered more than three hundred thousand cat mummies. Who knew that a catnap could last over two millennia?

Although these mummy makers of antiquity are the most famous of cat worshippers, this feline adoration has roots much deeper in the clay and soil of culture. Like anthropologists searching through bone fragments for a narrative of physical evolution, we too, dear reader, journey through these pages in search of origins. We long to see a distant relative, brushing the mane of a great Persian cat, blurred by the sands of time. Where did it all begin? Who was the first cat man?

Imagine, if you will, a cave in prehistoric France. A shaman sketches out the figure of a fierce cat with ash, spit, and dried berries on the rough stone walls. A torch flickers throughout the darkened cavern, and the crude images take on a striking likeness. Is it the hashish-induced madness of the onlooker? Could this be the moment of divine alchemy that spawned the first cat man?

Any history is largely a story of individuals. This book, as a collection of characters, is certain to leave out a number of important figures. Indeed, there are many players in Cat Land, and some omissions might even be deemed scandalous. However, parties are best kept small—enough people for lively conversation, but not overly loud and crowded.

While we as cat men, dear reader, are not all united in virtue—though, let's face it, many of us are—we all share a common sensibility. Though we have spent many years as a silent population, we all believe in the cat as a force for change in male consciousness—a secular embrace of an ancient religion.

Too often, those of our number peek out of the cat closet, grasping for images of ourselves, asking, "Is this normal?" "Am I a freak?" "What will my friends and family think?" Quell your fears, sir. In between these pages, you are among friends.

IN ANCIENT TIMES CATS WERE WORSHIPPED AS GODS; THEY HAVE NOT FORGOTTEN THIS.

Terry Pratchett

KING HYWEL *the* GOOD

TENTH-CENTURY WELSH KING

Our tale of cat men begins in the Dark Ages, a bleak time for pretty much everything even vaguely comfortable and civilized in the Western world. For cats, in particular, this was a violent age of superstition and ailurophobia. However, as we are well aware, cats are territorial, regal beasts, so it's fitting we begin in the court of the old kings of the British Isles.

Beginning around AD 920, the medieval king Hywel Dda ruled over much of present-day Wales. After visiting Rome as a young man, Hywel returned to his kingdom and set about bringing order to traditional Welsh law. Hywel the Good, as he is now known, introduced laws to protect domestic cats. Because Hywel recognized that cats were of great value to agriculture and the community as pest controllers, he introduced a scale of prices for kittens and cats that included penalties for killing or stealing a cat. These prices varied from one to four pence according to the age and killing ability of each cat.

Perhaps you wonder if merely placing monetary value on cats makes King Hywel the Good a cat man proper? By placing value on animals, Hywel afforded them protection through law. Considering this was a time when the touch of a king was thought to cure various maladies, such proto–animal rights laws were fairly sophisticated, and certainly deserving of our appreciation.

SULTAN BAIBARS

THIRTEENTH-CENTURY SULTAN

Long after the ancient Egyptians built temples to their feline-faced goddesses, the cat continued to be held in high regard by the Near Eastern cultures of antiquity. In particular, the cat is venerated in Islamic tradition for its cleanliness and for being loved by the Prophet Muhammad.

In the thirteenth century, a Mamluk sultan named Baibars ruled present-day Egypt. Much like today, large numbers of cats roamed the streets of medieval Cairo. Ever the cat man, Baibars bequeathed in his will a garden near his mosque for the benefit and protection of the cats of Cairo. According to British scholar Edward William Lane, "Every afternoon, a quantity of offal is brought into the great court before the Mahkemeh; and the cats are called together to eat."

While Baibars's ruling European counterparts killed cats en masse on account of satanic hysteria, Baibars's feline stewardship provided the cats of Cairo with sustenance and shelter for several centuries, a legacy underscoring the relationship between cats and Islam.

MICHEL *de* MONTAIGNE

PHILOSOPHER AND ESSAYIST

Throughout the last four hundred years, Michel de Montaigne has been regarded as one of the most influential writers of the French Renaissance. An aristocrat and statesman, Montaigne experienced a profound midlife crisis and began writing his much-famed essays.

For all intents and purposes, Michel de Montaigne invented the essay—and not the dreaded essays born of procrastination we remember from our school days. Derived from the French word *essai*, meaning "to try," "to attempt," the essays Montaigne wrote were candid explorations into his own psyche. His digressive style left few subjects untouched, from marriage and horseback riding to kidney stones and the proper way to leave a dinner party.

Given the breadth of subject matter he explored in his essays, it's no surprise that there is a particularly regarded passage in "An Apology for Raymond Sebond" about Montaigne's pet cat. In the essay, Montaigne writes critically of the vain tendency of humans to feel superior to animals. Wondering what the world might look like from her point of view, he writes, "When I play with my cat, how do I know she is not playing with me?" By imagining the world from the perspective of the other (another species, in this instance), he saw the world through the eyes of a thoroughly modern man—the *first* modern man, some might say. Cherished in the hundreds of years since their publication, Montaigne's essays helped lay the foundation for the Enlightenment in Europe. To be sure, his words will make us mindful of our cat's wide-eyed stare the next time we reach for a stuffed mouse.

WHEN I AM PLAYING WITH MY CAT, HOW DO I KNOW SHE IS NOT PLAYING WITH ME?

Michel de Montaigne

SIR ISAAC NEWTON

SCIENTIST

What else can be said about the father of modern science? Aside from his gorgeous locks of powdered hair and penchant for falling apples, Newton brought us laws of motion and universal gravitation that echo through the great halls of knowledge to this day. The man invented calculus, for crying out loud! Indeed, the inscription on his tomb at Westminster Abbey holds nothing back: *Mortals rejoice that there has existed such and so great an ornament of the human race!*

Alongside his list of accomplishments, there are a few notable mysteries. Number one on our list, dear reader, is a long-contested tale: Did Newton invent the first cat flap?

The story goes that Newton was conducting light experiments in a dark attic. When his cat kept disturbing him by pawing open the door, Newton allegedly cut a hole in the door to allow easy access for his demanding feline. In another version of the story, after his cat had kittens, Newton cut two holes in his door: a large one for the mother and a smaller for the kittens. It did not occur to him that the second hole was unnecessary, as the kittens would follow the mother through the larger door.

Now is this story true? It's debatable. Does this invention come close to his invention of calculus? That is for you to decide. Regardless, even speculation on the great Sir Isaac Newton's taste in cats certainly deserves mention.

SAMUEL JOHNSON

WRITER, CRITIC, LEXICOGRAPHER

You know you've made it as a public intellectual when a period of literature bears your name. The Age of Johnson, also known as the Age of Sensibility, is so-called because of the titanic influence of the writer, critic, and lexicographer Samuel Johnson.

Described as "arguably the most distinguished man of letters in English history," Samuel Johnson is best known for his colossal work, *A Dictionary of the English Language*, published in 1755. Although not the first dictionary printed, it was for nearly 150 years considered the most authoritative—replaced only by the *Oxford English Dictionary* beginning in 1884. The man *literally defined* the word *cat*.

As is fitting for a person of such accomplishment and intelligence, Johnson was a feline enthusiast. In his massively influential biography of Johnson, James Boswell makes special mention of one cat in particular that monopolized Johnson's affections. Hodge, as the cat was called, received gushing treatment by Johnson. Indeed, as Johnson's neighbor commented in his memoirs, he had "frequently seen the ruggedness of Dr. Johnson softened to smiles, and caresses; by the inarticulate, yet pathetic expressions of his favourite Hodge." Boswell also mentions Johnson venturing out on his own to buy oysters for Hodge, "lest the servants having that trouble should take a dislike to the poor creature."

Outside of Samuel Johnson's former home in London—now a museum— one is greeted by a statue not of Johnson the man, but of his beloved feline, Hodge, sitting atop an open dictionary, next to a pair of empty oyster shells. A fitting monument for a man of letters and his beloved cat.

I HAVE MY FAVORITE CAT, WHO IS ALSO MY PAPERWEIGHT, ON MY DESK WHILE I AM WRITING.

Ray Bradbury

EDWARD LEAR

AUTHOR AND ARTIST

Most people build their careers by making sense of the world—taking the messy, chaotic stuff of everyday life and organizing it into predictable patterns. However, there are also those who choose to go against the grain, mixing the predictable into strange combinations, resulting in delightful, consumable forms of nonsense. Edward Lear, poet and illustrator, is famous for such nonsense. His illustrated books compress silly, ribald thoughts into the neat packaging of limerick poetry.

The youngest of twenty-one children, Lear was a sickly child, suffering from epileptic seizures from the age of six to adulthood. He gained early renown for his paintings of birds and was employed as an ornithological draftsman for the Zoological Society of London. In 1846, Lear published *A Book of Nonsense*, an illustrated collection of limericks. It was a resounding success, popularizing the limerick form.

Lear's seemingly charmed adult life was marked by long periods of depression, which he referred to as "the Morbids." A salve for Lear's "Morbids" was his cat, Foss, his most valued companion near the end of his life. Countless drawings of and references to Foss are found in Lear's famous letters. From his descriptions, it's known that Foss had half a tail. Legend has it that a superstitious servant cut it off to prevent the cat from running away. It doesn't take a rocket scientist to assume this had the opposite of the desired effect.

In another wonderful anecdote, when Lear moved, he asked his architect to replicate the layout of his old house so as not to upset his sensitive pet Foss.

MARK TWAIN

WRITER AND WIT

If this collection of cat men were organized like a high school yearbook, American writer Mark Twain (né Samuel Clemens) would easily win "Most Quoted" in the list of superlatives—and probably "Best Mustache," too. Twain is one of the great wits of the nineteenth century, in an age noted for its great wit. Called "the father of American literature" by William Faulkner, Twain wrote novels that remain perennial classics.

In the canon of Twain quotations, there is a sizable cache of quips about cats. A consummate ailurophile, Twain at one point kept as many as eleven cats on his farm in Connecticut. Some of his fabulous beasts' names include Sour Mash, Apollinaris, Zoroaster, Blatherskite, and Beelzebub.

In one story, Twain was watching his daughter's cat while she was away convalescing in a sanatorium—as one did in 1905. This distinguished-looking black cat quickly became a favorite of Twain's. Bambino, as he was called, was living with Twain in New York when he disappeared one day. After initial searches turned up nothing, Twain took out an ad in the *New York American* newspaper, offering a reward for his safe return.

In an account from Twain's house servant Katy Leary, a stream of New Yorkers bearing cats showed up at Twain's door. A few days later, however, Bambino was found meowing across the street and brought home. According to Leary, "Mr. Clemens was delighted and then he advertised that his cat was found! But the people kept coming just the same with all kinds of cats for him—anything to get a glimpse of Mr. Clemens!"

A HOME WITH

AND A WELL-FED, WELL

REVERED CAT — MAY

perh

BUT HOW CAN

OUT A CAT—

—PETTED, AND PROPERLY

BE A PERFECT HOME,

aps,

IT PROVE TITLE?

Mark Twain

NIKOLA TESLA

We often speak of the creative spark—that moment when an idea is born with a figurative flicker or flash. For Nikola Tesla, inspiration took the form of a lightning bolt. As an inventor, electrical engineer, physicist, futurist, and overall super-genius, Tesla is credited for his expansion of alternating current designs. However, he may be best known for the cultish aura surrounding his late career research—his *unknown* inventions, if you will. At six foot three and slender in build, Tesla strikes an unlikely image of a mad scientist. But he was a genius *and* a gentleman, and his dapper dress and love of poetry stand in stark contrast to visions of a Dr. Frankenstein–esque fellow.

Like many persons of genius, Tesla was a sickly child. He claimed to have experienced profound visions, often preceded by blinding flashes of light. As an adult, he would experience vivid flashbacks to these experiences in his childhood. It is Tesla the boy genius that gains admission into the coven of cat men. In his writing *A Story of Youth Told by Age*, Tesla attributes his early interest in electricity to his beloved pet cat, Macak. On a cold, dry winter evening, Tesla stroked the furry coat of his cat, producing shocks of static electricity. "Macak's back was a sheet of light and my hand produced a shower of sparks loud enough to be heard all over the house," he observed.

This *aha* moment was a manifestation of scientific fact. Appearing almost supernatural in their vision, Tesla's ideas continue to capture popular imagination to this day. Just think, the Tesla coil—that bizarre futuristic monument to the mad scientist—all started with a little spark from a house cat in Croatia.

MAURICE RAVEL

COMPOSER

Cats isn't the only musical performance to feature spandex-clad felines. In an epic pairing of formidable ailurophiles, composer Maurice Ravel and novelist Colette collaborated on the opera *L'Enfant et les Sortilèges*. In the production, two feline lovers emerge from shadows, canoodling and meowing operatically. They rub against each other, moaning and occasionally hissing when the passion becomes too much to bear. More than just kinky cosplay, this bizarre duet provides a glimpse into the composer's secret life as a cat man.

Maurice Ravel is considered one of the main figures of the impressionist movement in music, known for his repetitive masterpiece *Boléro*. Born in France to a Basque mother and a Swiss inventor father—who was the creator of the notorious circus attraction the "Whirlwind of Death"— young Maurice started taking piano lessons at the age of six. Finding success at flaunting conservative musical traditions, Ravel rejected the bohemian aesthetic of Left Bank Paris. A slight, elegantly dressed dandy, he was, as one of his biographers claims, "among the first to wear pastel colored shirts in France."

Finding it nearly impossible to work in Paris after the First World War, he purchased a villa in a sleepy village west of the city. The narrow house, decorated with blue stripes, checkerboard floors, and Japanese antiques, was home to his two Siamese cats. The Siamese breed is known for their distinct, almost human meow, known as a "meezer." Ravel must have appreciated the musicality and occasional dissonance of his beloved cats' throaty calls. From atop the piano, the cats served as muses for one France's most important composers of the twentieth century.

LOUIS WAIN

ILLUSTRATOR

Few people have envisioned the cat through the same psychedelic lens as Victorian illustrator Louis Wain. Conflicting reports exist of when Wain became interested in drawing cats. In his obituary from 1939, his sister claims he began drawing kittens after he received one as a child. In another story, Wain began drawing his house cat, Peter, to comfort his dying wife. Regardless, his images of dandyish cats playing golf, smoking cigarettes, and strumming banjos became enormously successful. He became known as "The Man Who Draws Cats" and was eventually elected president of Britain's National Cat Club.

Wain's success coincided with the Victorian public's growing interest in "cat fancy," beginning with the first national cat show in 1871. As widely popular as his illustrations became—appearing in newspapers, books, and calendars—Wain's career suffered from a combination of poor financial decisions and declining mental health. By 1925, he was completely destitute, living in the pauper ward of a psychiatric hospital, diagnosed as schizophrenic. Wain's paintings of cats changed dramatically as his mental state worsened. In his later paintings— which later amassed a cult following—his once fluffy, doe-eyed felines are transformed into psychedelic bursts of pulsating rays. As knowledge of his condition became public, H. G. Wells—a cat man himself—and the prime minister of England helped secure Wain's transfer to a more commodious institution.

H. G. Wells said of him, "He has made the cat his own. He invented a cat style, a cat society, a whole cat world. English cats that do not look and live like Louis Wain cats are ashamed of themselves."

SIR WINSTON CHURCHILL

POLITICIAN

Winston Churchill is one of the most legendary statesmen of the modern era. As British prime minister during the Second World War, he led his country through harrowing battles and blitzes; his brilliant oration inspired public confidence during the bleakest moments of the war. He was called "The British Bulldog," both for his pugnacious attitude and for his oft-caricatured scowl. That a man thought to embody a canine spirit be included in a roster of cat lovers—often thought of as a foppish bunch of poets, painters, and "indoor" types—is an irony that betrays the more refined aspects of Churchill's personality.

During Churchill's two terms at 10 Downing Street, his cats provided much-needed levity in the often intense environment. Over time, his coterie of cats—Tango, Mickey, and Nelson, to name a few—became known by guests as essential personnel. His affection for his cats provided a foil to the cigar-smoking, scotch-drinking, acerbic-witted badassery commonly associated with Churchill. This was a man who liked to eat dinner with his cats close by, sneaking them scraps of smoked salmon below the table when his wife wasn't looking—a man who liked to paint landscapes while his cats patrolled a sun-dappled English rose garden.

For his eighty-eighth birthday, Churchill was given a marmalade cat he called Jock. Jock lived with Churchill and his wife at their estate, Chartwell, until Churchill's death at the age of ninety. When Chartwell was turned over to the National Trust, the Churchill family arranged for Jock to have a permanent residence at the house. After Jock's death at the age of thirteen, he was replaced by Jock II as per the family's wishes. Visitors to Chartwell today can espy the latest in the line of ginger residents of the estate, Jock IV.

WHAT GREATER GIFT THAN THE LOVE OF A CAT?

Charles Dickens

T.S. ELIOT

POET

On a darkened stage, dancers cavort in leopard leotards. Wisps of face paint pucker and stretch as performers grin into a green spotlight. A tribe of dancer cats in unitards, the "Jellicles," crowd the stage and decide which one of their number will ascend to heaven, to be reincarnated. This is *Cats*, the musical by Andrew Lloyd Webber, based on a book of "light verse" by poet T. S. Eliot.

Thomas Stearns Eliot is one of modernist poetry's beloved grandfathers. His epic poems *The Waste Land* and *The Love Song of J. Alfred Prufrock* are steep mountains in the landscape of modernism—required reading for many an English major. Although his writing was seen as overly obscure by some of his contemporaries, there are lighter moments in Eliot's body of work.

In particular, Eliot created a fanciful collection of poems about cats entitled *Old Possum's Book of Practical Cats.* Originally written for his godchildren, these poems regale the reader with tales of eccentrically named cats: Mr. Mistoffelees, Skimbleshanks, Bustopher Jones, and Rum Tum Tugger, to name a few. In one long incantation of a poem, Eliot informs the reader about the proper way to name a cat. Originally published in 1939, the slim volume featured illustrations by Eliot himself. Later editions of this beloved book were illustrated by the likes of Edward Gorey (see page 75).

When writing about Eliot for a *Cats* theater program, his late wife revealed, "Whenever he was unwell or could not sleep, TSE would recite the verses under his breath." Now one of the longest-running musicals in history, *Cats* remains a testament to the infectious whimsy of Eliot's words and an enduring legacy of his feline muses.

PAUL KLEE

According to some animal behaviorists, house cats never really grow up. Through the domestication process, adult cats remain little Peter Pans, living in a permanent mental state of kittenhood. While some humans refuse to grow up—there's one in every family—there are those rare individuals who, as adults, attempt to channel the boundless imagination of childhood. For Swiss-born artist Paul Klee, the artwork of children served as a wellspring of inspiration for his inventive visual language and visionary paintings.

Originally trained as a violinist, Klee dedicated himself to painting as a teenager—first associated with the German Expressionist Blaue Reiter group and later with the Bauhaus school. Known as the "Bauhaus Buddha," Klee found inspiration everywhere in nature. Among his varied subject matter, Klee was often drawn to animals. Cats in particular found their way into a number of his better-known works. Throughout his life, Klee shared his home and studio with cats—first with Bimbo, then Fritzi (aka Fritzpoule), and then with Bimbo II.

In one anecdote, an American collector recalled visiting Klee's studio at the Bauhaus. In a room filled with hanging bits of glass and mobiles, Klee pulled out drawings while his cats milled about. As the collector was looking at a drawing, Klee's cat started walking across the paper. The collector attempted to shoo it away. "Oh, don't do that," Klee responded. The collector, perplexed, replied, "Well, it will make footprints all over the drawing." Klee, in his typical Zen fashion, responded, "I know. But one of you art historians will end up saying, 'How did he get that effect?'"

TSUGUHARU FOUJITA

ARTIST

In Paris in the 1920s, it would have been hard to miss the enigmatic painter of cats, Tsuguharu Foujita. His distinct, fashion-forward ensemble comprised a geometric bowl cut, large earrings, a wristwatch tattoo, a toothbrush moustache, and, occasionally, a toga accessorized with a lampshade hat. Needless to say, he cut quite a figure.

At the height of his fame, he was more successful than Picasso. However, like some of the brightest stars in the sky, this unforgettable, vivid individual seemed to fade as the years passed. Only recently is his work being resurrected from the annals of art history to a larger global audience.

Throughout his career, Foujita's aesthetic bridged East and West. Arriving in Paris from his native Japan in 1913, he quickly fit in with the bohemian scene in Montparnasse, sharing a studio with Amedeo Modigliani and Chaim Soutine. Much like the cats he painted, Foujita was famously known for his cleanliness. Though already well regarded by the artist set, he became incredibly popular with models after installing a bath with hot running water in his studio.

In terms of his work, his subject matter throughout his career was fairly consistent: self-portraits with cats, women with cats, and cats with other cats. In 1920, he produced twenty etchings of languid felines for *A Book of Cats*, a collection of poetry by Michael Joseph. Originally from an edition of five hundred, a copy recently sold at auction for nearly $80,000. It's certainly one of the rarest and most desired books on cats in existence. Besides this one, of course.

RAYMOND CHANDLER

WRITER

Every great city deserves a great detective. For London in the late Victorian era, it was Sherlock Holmes. For the thoroughly modern city of Los Angeles in mid-twentieth-century America, it was Philip Marlowe. Marlowe, the hard-boiled gumshoe created by novelist Raymond Chandler, was a bourbon-drinking knight in a land of neon signs and smoky hotel bars.

When Chandler arrived in Los Angeles in the 1920s, it was a new metropolis, a city without a past. This urban blank slate appealed to Chandler, who only began writing detective novels at the age of forty-four. Prior to this, he worked as an apricot picker, a tennis racket stringer, and an oil executive. A varied résumé, to say the least.

Throughout his writing career, Raymond Chandler was never far from his beloved cat, Taki, a black Persian whom he referred to as his secretary. Taki was originally spelled *Take*. However, Chandler grew tired of telling people she was named after the Japanese word for bamboo and thus pronounced with two syllables. He got Taki around the time he started writing novels. As Chandler wrote to a friend, she was a constant presence on his desk, "usually sitting on the paper I wanted to use . . . sometimes leaning up against the typewriter and sometimes just quietly gazing out of the window from a corner of the desk, as if to say, 'The stuff you're doing is a waste of time, bud.'"

I SAID SOMETHING WHICH

I HATED CATS.

I am one of the most fanatical

IF YOU HATE THEM, I

IF YOUR ALLERGIES HATE

SITUATION TO THE

GAVE YOU TO THINK

BUT GAD, SIR,

cat lovers in the business.

MAY LEARN TO HATE YOU.

THEM, I WILL TOLERATE THE

BEST OF MY ABILITY.

Raymond Chandler

GEORGE BALANCHINE

DANCER AND CHOREOGRAPHER

Generally speaking, cat men are not a stunningly athletic bunch. An agile-limbed ailurophile is a rare find, so it's with great pomp that we raise our glasses to Russian-born dancer and choreographer George Balanchine. Regarded as the father of American ballet, Balanchine is one of the most important figures in the world of ballet in the twentieth century.

Beginning his choreography career with the Ballets Russes in Paris, Balanchine moved to New York, where he and Lincoln Kirstein—another cat lover—cofounded the School of American Ballet and later the New York City Ballet. As intense as he was prolific, Balanchine created more than four hundred works during his lifetime. Famed for his "neoclassical style," Balanchine fused classical technique with a thoroughly modern sensibility. His performances, including his perennially popular version of Tchaikovsky's *The Nutcracker*, are classics of modern ballet.

As a teacher, Balanchine found that one of his most surprising star pupils was his beloved cat named Mourka. After a photo capturing the cat in midleap ran in *Life* magazine, Mourka became one of the first feline celebrities in America. Naturally, a book soon followed. *Mourka: The Autobiography of a Cat* was written by Balanchine's wife Tanaquil Le Clercq and photographed by Martha Swope. Narrated by Mourka, the pampered tan-and-white cat recalls his life's story, from meager beginnings at a shelter to learning *grand jetés* and the all-too-fitting *pas des chats* by the masterful Balanchine in his Upper West Side apartment.

According to one biographer, composer Igor Stravinsky was at a Christmas party at Balanchine's apartment and asked to see Mourka perform. As some guests later recalled, it was the only time Balanchine seemed nervous before a performance.

JEAN COCTEAU

Writer Colette once inscribed, "There are no ordinary cats." In this book, dear reader, there are no ordinary cat men. To be sure, *ordinary* is not how one would describe Colette's friend and neighbor Jean Cocteau. The French poet, filmmaker, artist, playwright, and novelist remains the dandy prince of modernism.

After leaving home at fifteen, Cocteau joined a bohemian circle in Paris and began publishing books of poetry. Ever the artistic polymath, he expanded into ballet, collaborating in 1917 with the legendary Ballets Russes on a work entitled *Parade*, with sets and costumes designed by Pablo Picasso and music by Erik Satie. From theater and dance, Cocteau made his foray into film, creating the surreal masterpieces *Beauty and the Beast* and *The Orphic Trilogy*.

Throughout Cocteau's expansive body of work, cats are a regular theme. He was a member of the Cat Friends Club in Paris—even designing the membership pin—and was often photographed with his feline friends. In his film *Beauty and the Beast*, the beast, as it were, is envisioned not as some terrifying wolflike creature, but is instead an overgrown Persian cat, resplendent in gold-trimmed gauchos and puffy-shouldered pantsuits.

In 1947, Cocteau purchased a stone house on the property of a château at Milly-la-Fôret in northern France. He renovated a derelict chapel from the twelfth century that was not far from the home. Inside, Cocteau painted dynamic murals of the crucifixion and lush flora, punctuated with cosmic and Masonic symbols in his characteristic contour line work. Near the corner of the entrance is a small painted cat, peering out from the mural. As per his request, Cocteau was buried in the chapel. Known as "The Frivolous Prince" in his life, Cocteau, like many cat-worshipping Egyptian royalty, is watched over throughout eternity by the keen stare of a cat.

I LOVE CATS BECAUSE I ENJOY MY HOME; AND LITTLE BY LITTLE THEY BECOME ITS VISIBLE SOUL.

Jean Cocteau

ERNEST HEMINGWAY

WRITER

Ernest Hemingway is popularly depicted as the archetypal macho writer. While he certainly embodied the most flamboyant features of masculinity—guns, booze, women, and big game hunting—Hemingway had a much softer side. Entombed within his great barrel chest was a cat man of epic proportions.

A member of the so-called Lost Generation (a term coined by writer Gertrude Stein), Hemingway moved to Paris as a journalist after World War I and joined a circle of literary expatriates, including Stein, F. Scott Fitzgerald, and James Joyce. Despite his connection to the urbane literati of Paris, Hemingway is most often associated with rugged adventure. His love of hunting, fishing, and bullfighting led him around the world, eventually owning homes in Key West, Florida, as well as Wyoming and Cuba.

While living in Key West, Hemingway was given a cat by a ship's captain. Snow White was a six-toed feline, the first of Hemingway's famous brood of polydactyl cats in Key West. Polydactyls are born with extra fingers and toes. For a human, this can be the addition of a digit or two. For cats, however, the math is much more impressive. The world record for extra cat toes belongs to Tiger, a twenty-seven-toed marvel.

As Papa Ernest not so famously said, "One cat just leads to another." In the case of our feline comrades, eighteen toes just lead to another nine. Hemingway's cats—or "purr factories" and "love sponges," as he was fond of calling them—reveal a softer, more nuanced portrait of Papa.

A CAT HAS ABSOLUTE EMOTIONAL HONESTY: HUMAN BEINGS,

for one reason or another,

MAY HIDE THEIR FEELINGS, BUT A CAT DOES NOT.

Ernest Hemingway

BALTHUS

PAINTER

Painter Balthasar Klossowski de Rola, simply known as Balthus, is one of the great enigmas of twentieth-century art. In fact, before his 1968 retrospective at the Tate in London, Balthus sent a telegram stating, "No biographical details. Begin: Balthus is a painter of whom nothing is known. Now let us look at the pictures. Regards, B."

From his vast chalet in Switzerland, Balthus quietly painted his large canvases, shrouding his personal and artistic life in mystery. His pictures are dreamlike narratives that have always courted a fair share of controversy, both disturbing and enchanting viewers with scenes of young girls reclining in amber-lit interiors.

His personal complexities and scandalous subject matter make him an uneasy figure to write about, dear reader. However, it's his love of cats, both as companions and as subject matter, that puts him between these pages.

At the age of eleven, Balthus created a series of ink paintings chronicling the discovery and tragic loss of a beloved stray cat. The resulting forty paintings formed the book *Mitsou*, published by German poet Rainer Maria Rilke. Years later, at the age of twenty-seven, he painted a nearly life-size self-portrait titled *The King of Cats*. Staring out from the canvas, his slight, dandylike figure stands with a hand on his hip while an outsize tortoiseshell feline rubs up against his chinos-clad legs.

Much has been made of the role of cats in Balthus's paintings. They're seen as a worldly foil to the girlish innocence of the models, or possibly a stand-in for the painter himself. Regardless, the cats of his paintings continue to haunt and beguile from their fixed place in museums across the world.

ROMARE BEARDEN

ARTIST

We assume that by now, it's abundantly clear from these biographical portraits that Cat men are multidimensional individuals. For American artist Romare Bearden, this is surely an understatement. Before becoming a titan of American art, he studied medicine, mathematics, and education; turned down a career in professional baseball; worked as a caseworker for the New York Department of Social Services; and, for a few years, was a professional songwriter.

First and foremost, Bearden was a born storyteller. Moving with his family from rural North Carolina to Harlem during the Great Migration, Bearden came of age during the Harlem Renaissance. Through careful snips of his scissors, he created bold, cubist collages with the studied improvisation of a jazz musician. Influenced by jazz, African folklore, Greek myths, and Dutch master paintings, Bearden used the African American experience as a lens for exploring universal themes.

Like many other refined fellows of arts and letters, Bearden was also known for his love of cats. His respect for his felines is evident in the distinguished names he gave them: Mikie was short for Michelangelo; Tuttle, short for Egyptian pharaoh Tutankhamen; and Rusty, after the hero of Persian mythology, Rustum. Such was Bearden's attachment to his cats that he and his wife would bring them along during their travels. On one of their voyages abroad, Bearden booked a separate room for two of his cats and hired someone to look after them.

Bearden was often photographed in his studio with his beloved tan-and-gray cat Gypo. In an interview, he mused that Gypo—a "natural ham"—could have had a career in cat food ads. The cat is a recurring motif in both the life and the work of this quintessentially American artist.

WILLIAM S. BURROUGHS

WRITER

In a gentleman's club such as this, there are bound to be a few scandals. When Beat Generation writer William S. Burroughs's novel *Naked Lunch* was published in 1962, it was the subject of what would be one of the last major obscenity trials for a work of literature in the United States. His gritty, drug-addled prose touched a nerve, revealing the paranoid shadow-self of booming postwar America. He was a revolutionary writer, gun enthusiast, junkie, and gay grandfather of the counterculture. However, amid the din of his much-discussed law-breaking exploits, there was a separate narrative playing out: the quiet story of Burroughs the cat man.

In many ways, Burroughs connected with cats more than people. His house in Lawrence, Kansas, was a virtual cat colony. For the Harvard-educated writer, cats were not only much-loved companions; they were also spiritual guides. Fletch, Ruski, and Smoke were a few of Burroughs's beloved familiars that tiptoed through his life like a poetic motif.

Near the end of his life, Burroughs wrote *The Cat Inside*, an auto-biographical novella exploring his life through the cats he'd lived with over the years. His writing is uncharacteristically vulnerable, and he credits cats with restoring his humanity. Burroughs was once asked by poet and fellow Beat Allen Ginsberg if he ever wanted to be loved. "It depends. By who or what," he said. "By my cats, certainly."

MY RELATIONSHIP WITH CATS HAS SAVED ME FROM A DEADLY, PERVASIVE IGNORANCE.

William S. Burroughs

SAUL STEINBERG

CARTOONIST AND ILLUSTRATOR

Animals are often said to resemble their owners (though, as any cat person will tell you, one can never "own" a cat). This popular sentiment is turned on its head in the drawings of cartoonist and illustrator Saul Steinberg. Many of the cats he drew throughout his meteoric career seem to resemble the artist himself: mustachioed and sporting a subtle grin. His drawings strike a balance of sophistication and play, much like the felines he portrayed.

After escaping Fascist Italy as a student of architecture, Steinberg eventually landed in New York, a city he would redefine again and again with his iconic covers for the *New Yorker*. A virtuoso draftsman with a razor-sharp wit, Steinberg was a charismatic man about town, finding success both in the pages of magazines and on the walls of galleries. His dandyish presence was perfectly suited to cocktail parties of the literati as well as to downtown gatherings of abstract painters.

Steinberg's drawings are landscapes of varied styles and density, peppered with skyscrapers, train tickets, crocodiles, period costumes, and, of course, cats. Such feline portrayals weren't limited to sheets of paper. He was known for creating masks out of brown paper bags and donning them for guests, as well as for drawing directly on chairs, stools, and bathtubs. A number of these playful experiments are homages to his beloved spirit animal.

Steinberg had several cats throughout his life, but his last cat, Papoose, was certainly the dearest. Living off and on with Steinberg in his Hamptons home, the black tuxedo cat was a loyal companion. After the passing of Papoose, Steinberg reflected in his diary on his furry friend's virtues: "Courage, grace and dignity, a true man."

CHARLES BUKOWSKI

POET

Dubbed the "laureate of American lowlife" by *Time* magazine, poet and writer Charles Bukowski is adored around the world for his free-verse odes to hard drinking, womanizing, and good old-fashioned brawling. His is a poetry of hard living. Whereas John Keats wrote about his famed Grecian urn, Bukowski wrote odes to the proverbial ashtray, musing about the less refined aspects of human life—subject matter not often broached in poetry.

After a decade spent drifting and drinking around America, a stint working at a pickle factory, and many years working for the U.S. Postal Service, Bukowski began writing full-time at the age of forty-nine. He was extremely prolific, publishing more than twenty books of poetry in his lifetime, not to mention dozens of chapbooks, novels, and screenplays. Weaving in and out of the sometimes violent, gritty, and occasionally sweet stanzas are dozens of cats. Some nap in the sun, while other lurk under cars, feasting on birds. Whatever their activity, Bukowski's cats are survivors—self-sufficient and wise.

As Bukowski got older, he lived in a house in the suburbs of Los Angeles with his wife and their many cats. At this later stage in life, his writing about cats became much more sentimental, a far cry from his rough-and-tumble reputation. In an interview shortly before his death, Bukowski advised, "If you're feeling bad, you just look at the cats, you'll feel better, because they know that everything is, just as it is. There's nothing to get excited about. They just know. They're saviours. The more cats you have, the longer you live. If you have a hundred cats, you'll live ten times longer than if you have ten. Someday this will be discovered, and people will have a thousand cats and live forever. It's truly ridiculous."

IN MY NEXT LIFE
I WANT TO BE A CAT.
TO SLEEP TWENTY HOURS
A DAY AND WAIT TO BE FED.
TO SIT AROUND LICKING
MY ASS.

Charles Bukowski

MARLON BRANDO

ACTOR

Gentlemen may prefer blondes, but Wild Ones prefer cats. The brooding, complex character of Marlon Brando casts a long shadow in the history of cinema. Brilliant and mercurial, Brando's acting performances—from *On the Waterfront* and *A Streetcar Named Desire* to *Last Tango in Paris*, to name a few—continue to outshine his often tempestuous personal life. His love for cats, in particular, both softens and complicates his macho image.

Marlon Brando's penchant for felines helped shape one of the most iconic characters in film history. In the opening scene of *The Godfather*, Vito Corleone calmly pets a cat while doling out favors on the day of his daughter's wedding. The cat was not originally written into the script. Director Francis Ford Coppola allegedly found the gray tabby wandering around the lot at Paramount Studios and, in an inspired moment, gave it to Brando before the cameras started rolling. Although Brando was most pleased by the furry addition, the cat's purring was so loud that many of The Don's lines had to be overdubbed.

However, well before the dawn of The Don, Brando's affection for cats was documented in a series of publicity shots. In the mid-1950s, Brando was photographed in his Los Angeles home hanging out with his beloved cat. The photos show Brando reclining on his couch with his pet sleeping on his shoulders as he worked at his typewriter. Such images offer a rare glimpse into the personal life of this reclusive icon.

EDWARD GOREY

The macabre genius of author and illustrator Edward Gorey brings to mind images of haunted orphanages and untimely demises. Nothing is as it seems; rugs hide monsters and even alphabets aren't to be trusted. Throughout his career, Gorey wrote and illustrated more than a hundred books, and designed sets for the ballet, theater, and animation. In both his work and his personal life, Gorey the man is remembered for his profound love of cats.

His home on Cape Cod was a veritable paradise for cats. Famously cluttered with stacks of books—more than twenty-five thousand by some estimates—handmade stuffed animals, antique furniture, and found objets d'art, Gorey's cats lived and napped in a well-read, if not slightly decrepit, jungle gym. Though the numbers fluctuated over the years, he typically lived with around six cats, many of them named after characters from the Japanese classic *The Tale of Genji*.

Gorey was famous for donning fur coats—he was often seen draped in raccoon pelts at performances of the New York City Ballet. Whether these were worn in solidarity with his feline friends, we'll never know. However, as Gorey grew older, he became conflicted about his passion for fur, eventually putting his collection of coats in storage. Upon his death in 2000, Gorey left his entire estate to a charitable trust for the welfare of cats and dogs, as well as bats and insects. In 2010, his collection of fur coats was auctioned off in New York, with the proceeds supporting animal charities. His home on Cape Cod is now a museum celebrating Gorey's life, work, and passion for animals.

ANDY WARHOL

ARTIST

Long before the quaalude-induced blur that was The Factory, Andy Warhol was an illustrator working in New York. After leaving his working-class Pittsburgh home for the Big City, he lived in a cramped Upper East Side apartment, gaining a reputation for his drawings of shoes for department stores. In the early Fifties, Julia Warhola, Andy's doting mother, left Pittsburgh to live with her son. Much like a scene from *Grey Gardens*, mother and son lived in squalid glamour in their tiny New York apartment.

Along with a love of drawing, Andy and Julia shared a deep fondness for cats. As told by Warhol's nephew, James Warhola, in his book *Uncle Andy's Cats*, Warhol received a kitten from actress Gloria Swanson. Hester, as she was called, had a litter of kittens with Warhol's other cat, Sam. From this initial litter grew a large brood of cats, each one named Sam. Eventually, their number topped fifteen, making Andy and Julia's (now much larger) brownstone a virtual cat colony of little Sams.

In 1954, Warhol and his mother collaborated on an illustrated book of cats. Andy's bold watercolors and decorative line work were complemented by his mother's whimsical calligraphy. The resulting work was a limited-edition book called *25 Cats Name Sam and One Blue Pussy*. When Julia penned the title, she forgot the *d* in *named*. Warhol, who was always interested in artistic imperfections, liked the mistake and kept it in.

Warhol's superstar legacy, as we all know, managed to far outlast his oft-repeated fifteen minutes of fame. Judging by the auction results of an original *25 Cats Name Sam and One Blue Pussy* book in 2013—fetching more than $40,000—the star power of his famous cats isn't going anywhere either.

KARL LAGERFELD

DESIGNER

Fashion designers are well known for their intense, albeit fleeting relationships with muses. For the legendary designer and creative director of Chanel, Karl Lagerfeld, his muse is a pampered, long-haired Siamese cat named Choupette (which means "sweetie" in French).

At age seventy-seven, Lagerfeld was christened a cat man late in life. Starting out as a self-described dog person, Lagerfeld fell in love with Choupette while cat-sitting for a friend. Since then, he has spared no time—and expense—becoming a cat man extraordinaire. When Lagerfeld is home in Paris, Choupette eats lunch and dinner with him on designer dishware. She has two personal maids who record her activities, behavior, meals, and temperament in a daily journal. In her first nine months, they had written more than six hundred pages of entries.

Pampered though she may be, Choupette is far from being a furry layabout; she's a working girl. The unofficial brand ambassador of Chanel, Choupette has social media accounts with tens of thousands of followers. In her book, *Choupette: The Private Life of a High-Flying Fashion Cat*, she—through interpretation of Lagerfeld and others—advises readers on fashion, travel, and luxury living. As a model, she made three million euros from just two modeling gigs in 2014. Eat your heart out, Linda Evangelista.

Lagerfeld admits Choupette's a kept woman, and has stated he would marry her if it were legal.

I NEVER THOUGHT I WOULD FALL IN LOVE LIKE THIS WITH A CAT.

Karl Lagerfeld

FREDDIE MERCURY

MUSICIAN

Possessing a four-octave range and flamboyant style both on and off stage, Freddie Mercury remains one of the most distinctive rock stars of the twentieth century. Born Farrokh Bulsara, he changed his name to Freddie Mercury soon after joining Queen, presumably in anticipation of his galactic rise to fame.

Mercury was a cat man of the first order, deeply dedicated to his feline family throughout his life. His brood of cats included Oscar, Delilah, Miko, Romeo, and Goliath. Delilah was particularly dear to Mercury, making her the namesake and subject matter of a song from Queen's 1991 album *Innuendo*.

While away on tour, Mercury was known to call his best friend who was watching his cats, asking to speak to them over the phone. She would put the phone to their furry ears to hear his voice. Mercury was known for spoiling his friends and loved ones with extravagant gifts, and his cats were no exception. They each received home-cooked meals of meat and fish and were given individual Christmas stockings, brimming over with treats and toys.

As Mercury's health began to deteriorate, his cats were of great comfort to him. In his last known portrait, Mercury is pictured sporting a silk vest, boldly painted with depictions of his feline friends. After his life was tragically cut short by AIDS in 1991, his cats continued to live with Mercury's best friend in his London home. For years afterward, some fans claimed to have seen Delilah perched on a windowsill, no doubt looking at the stars, searching for Mercury, that brightest of fleeting lights in the night sky.

HARUKI MURAKAMI

WRITER

A missing cat is a terrible thing, dear reader. And an unexpected journey into the underworld isn't much more desirable. However, for superstar Japanese novelist Haruki Murakami, either scenario is an occasion for a metaphysical reading experience. Murakami's stories lead the reader to the bottoms of wells, isolated libraries, and interdimensional hotels. Men can talk to cats and cats respond in kind.

For being one of the most internationally renowned novelists of his generation, Murakami the man is mysterious. He began writing at the age of forty. Prior to that, he owned a jazz club and coffeehouse in Tokyo, aptly named the Peter Cat. Notoriously reclusive, Murakami has composed many of his beloved novels in the company of his feline familiars—Kirin, Butch, Sundance, Mackerel, and Scotty, to name a few.

In his novel *Kafka on the Shore*, one of the protagonists is a character named Nakata, who, after suffering total amnesia as a child as the result of an extraterrestrial experience, has the ability to speak to cats. In another story called "Town of Cats," from his weighty novel *1Q84*, a man finds himself marooned overnight in a town populated with cats. The man hides in a bell tower and witnesses the large cats' nocturnal lives: going to work in their offices, shopping at the pharmacy, and drinking in bars.

In January 2015, Murakami created a temporary website in which he fielded questions from his fans. Thousands of readers sent in their queries about love, writing, and, of course, cats. When one reader asked for advice on finding his lost cat, Murakami replied, "Cats just disappear sometimes. You have to love and appreciate them while they're near you."

I LOVED TO READ; I LOVED TO
LISTEN TO MUSIC; AND I
LOVED CATS. THOSE THREE
THINGS. SO, EVEN THOUGH
I WAS AN ONLY KID,
I COULD BE HAPPY BECAUSE
I KNEW WHAT I LOVED.

Haruki Murakami

AI WEIWEI

Cats, unlike dogs, are not pack animals. They don't conform easily. Like wild hair in an otherwise majestic mane, a typical cat has a rebellious streak.

In the world of humans, artists are often famed for their similarly defiant attitude. In the case of renowned Chinese artist Ai Weiwei, he has channeled this rebellious nature into a multidisciplinary studio practice that blurs the line between art and political activism. He tackles issues like government corruption, censorship, and mishandled national tragedies. Weiwei's use of social media has bolstered his reputation as both an artist and an activist. Naturally, like many of us, cat photos appear regularly in his posts. For Weiwei, who has been imprisoned numerous times by the Chinese government, these lighthearted moments provide a counterpoint to his confrontational subject matter.

In Weiwei's home and studio in Beijing, more than forty cats roam the grounds. They walk across worktables, brushing against sculpture maquettes, and sunbathe in his courtyard, surrounded by Weiwei's enormous, multicolored vases. In Alison Klayman's 2012 documentary, *Ai Weiwei: Never Sorry*, Weiwei watches as a precocious cat jumps up to unlatch a door, opening it to the outdoor courtyard. Weiwei muses, "Only one cat has the ability to open doors. If I didn't have this cat, I would never have known that cats could open doors." That one cat out of forty could rebel, break free, and challenge a system—open a door— is a fitting metaphor for the fiercely independent Weiwei.

THE CAT COULD VERY WELL BE
MAN'S BEST FRIEND,
BUT WOULD NEVER
STOOP TO ADMITTING IT.

Doug Larson

ON ROBOTS and CATS

In 2012, intent on making a machine with the ability to learn on its own, Google engineers created an artificial brain of sorts by connecting sixteen thousand computer processors and exposing the network to a steady diet of YouTube images—over ten million in total. And what, after three days, did this cyborg brain learn to do? Recognize cats, naturally. The "neural network" was able to identify cats absent any telling information provided by the project programmers. If indulging in cat videos sounds like your lunch break, you may have more in common with robots than you realize. It appears that even robotic minds have cats on the brain.

Although it is imperative that we look backward in history to see where we as cat men originated, we must also consider what the future holds, dear reader. Ray Kurzweil, noted futurist, inventor, and fellow cat enthusiast, has made a career of thinking about the future. In particular, he has written extensively on his concept of the *singularity*: the point when artificial intelligence will surpass human intelligence.

If the singularity prophecy comes to pass, will the future cat men be cyborgs? Will their feline companions require software updates? Will whiskers pick up Wi-Fi signals? *Who will the future cat men be?* This brave new world will continue to place challenges on our sense of humanity. Our ability to relax without distraction, to allow ourselves to be bored and to appreciate quiet contemplation, will be stressed as we march toward a more technologically infused existence.

The pressure of our digital lives can sometimes lead many of us to dream of unplugging totally, of adopting a vaguely druidic wardrobe, changing our names to Dreamweaver or Fennel, and learning to craft bespoke sundials. However, before being consumed by Luddite paranoia, we must acknowledge that technology has made us cat men, and cat people in general, connected as never before. At present, the feline species is going through a kind of renaissance. The Internet has become a proverbial dog park for cat people. Once isolated from each other, we can now share our favorite pictures of our whiskered shut-ins with the world. Now, as ever, the cat's status in culture continues to evolve, thrive, and abide.

When mummified citizens were entombed in ancient Egypt, cats were buried with them as companions on their journey to the next world. The cat has always been a threshold dweller—a creature that exists between worlds. Just like its divine Egyptian ancestor, the cat of the future walks beside us as we wander toward a distant doorway.

Throughout the centuries, cat men have been quiet innovators and visionaries. From our libraries, studios, workshops, or sofas, we continue to learn from our feline friends—learn to relax into an afternoon nap; learn to elevate idleness to an art form. Like the Egyptian carver sculpting the figure of Bastet in stone, we still try to capture and understand the mysterious feline spirit. In our attempt to understand our cats, we in fact discover ourselves, more gentlemanly and, dare I say, more human.

ABOUT THE AUTHOR

SAM KALDA is an illustrator living and working in Brooklyn. His illustrations have appeared in places such as the *New York Times*, *Wall Street Journal*, and Vogue.com, as well as on products at West Elm. His work has been exhibited in New York, Los Angeles, and Berlin and has been recognized by American Illustration and the Society of Illustrators. See more of it at samkalda.com.

ACKNOWLEDGMENTS

Many thanks to my fabulous editor, Kaitlin Ketchum, and art director extraordinaire, Betsy Stromberg, from Ten Speed Press. You have been the best team a first-time author could ask for.

I began this project in the first year of my MFA at the Fashion Institute of Technology and owe much of its development to my time spent there. Special thanks to Melanie Reim, Dennis Dittrich, and Rudy Gutierrez, as well as my classmates—especially Julie Muszynski for her sharp eye and thoughtful advice.

Additional thanks to Catherine Boutwell and Joe Charap for their warm meals and generosity of spirit. To my friends and colleagues who provided feedback and encouragement, I am grateful indeed.

As always, love and thanks to my parents, Laurie and Ellison, for essentially everything, as well as the Kalda Kids (Emily, Jake, Molly, and Maggie). You're my favorite people in the world.

To my beloved cat, Sister, for ensuring my productivity with her 6 a.m. right-hook wakeup calls. To Lily, Patches, and all the other cats who have led me here—may the fallen among you sunbathe eternally in Elysian Fields of catnip. And to Phoebe, a fine dog and fellow cat lover.

Finally, thanks to Dan, my husband and "partner" in the truest sense of the word. To quote Jack Palance in *Batman*, "You are my number one guy."

SOURCES

Bair, Deirdre. *Saul Steinberg*. New York: Nan A. Talese, 2012.

Bakewell, Sarah. *How to Live, Or, a Life of Montaigne: One Question and Twenty Attempts at an Answer.* New York: Other Press, 2010.

Burroughs, William S. *The Cat Inside*. New York: Viking, 1992.

Chandler, Raymond, *Raymond Chandler Speaking*. Edited by Dorothy Gardiner and Kathrine Sorely Walker. Berkeley: University of California Press, 1977.

Cummings, Paul. "Oral history interview with Edward M. M. Warburg." *Archives of American Art*, Smithsonian Institution (May 13, 1971).

Denham, Sidney. "From the archive, 5 August 1960: The man who drew cats." *The Guardian* (August 5, 2013). http://www.theguardian.com/theguardian/2013/aug/05/cats-louis-wain-illustrations.

Devers, A. N. "The Coats of Edward Gorey." *The Daily* (blog), *The Paris Review* (January 4, 2011), http://www.theparisreview.org/blog/2011/01/04/the-coats-of-edward-gorey.

Durden-Smith, Jo. "Lost Art." *Departures* (March 30, 2010). http://www.departures.com/letters/features/lost-art.

Ghent, Henri. "Oral history interview with Romare Bearden." *Archives of American Art*, Smithsonian Institution (June 29, 1969).

Glueckstein, Fred. "Churchill's Feline Menagerie." The Churchill Centre (2008). http://www.winstonchurchill.org/support?catid=0&id=837.

Hall, Donald. "T. S. Eliot, The Art of Poetry No. 1." *The Paris Review* 21 (1959).

Leyser, Yony. "The Cat Offers Itself." *VICE* (October 1, 2012). https://www.vice.com/read/the-cat-offers-itself-0000360-v19n9.

Orenstein, Arbie. *Ravel: Man and Musician.* Mineola: Dover Publications, 1975.

Papova, Maria. "Literary Pets: The Cats, Dogs, and Birds Authors Loved." *Brainpickings* (April 29, 2013). https://www.brainpickings.org/2013/04/29/literary-pets.

Penn, Sean. "Tough Guys Write Poetry: Charles Bukowski." *Interview Magazine* (September 1987).

Rogers, Katherine. *The Cat and the Human Imagination.* Ann Arbor: University of Michigan Press, 2001.

Taper, Bernard. *Balanchine, A Biography*. Berkeley: University of California Press, 1996.

Updike, John. "Subconscious Tunnels," review of *Kafka on the Shore* by Haruki Murakami. *The New Yorker* (January 24, 2005). http://www.newyorker.com/magazine/2005/01/24/subconscious-tunnels.

Vircondelet, Alain. *Balthus and Cats*. Paris: Flammarion, 2013.

Warhola, James. *Uncle Andy's Cats*. New York: G.P. Putnam's Sons, 2009.

Copyright © 2017 by Sam Kalda

All rights reserved.
Published in the United States by Ten Speed Press,
an imprint of the Crown Publishing Group, a division
of Penguin Random House LLC, New York.
www.crownpublishing.com
www.tenspeed.com

Ten Speed Press and the Ten Speed Press colophon are
registered trademarks of Penguin Random House LLC.

Library of Congress Cataloging-in-Publication Data
is on file with the publisher.

Hardcover ISBN: 978-0-399-57844-1
eBook ISBN: 978-0-399-57845-8

Printed in China

Design by Betsy Stromberg

10 9 8 7 6 5 4 3 2 1

First Edition